I0760240

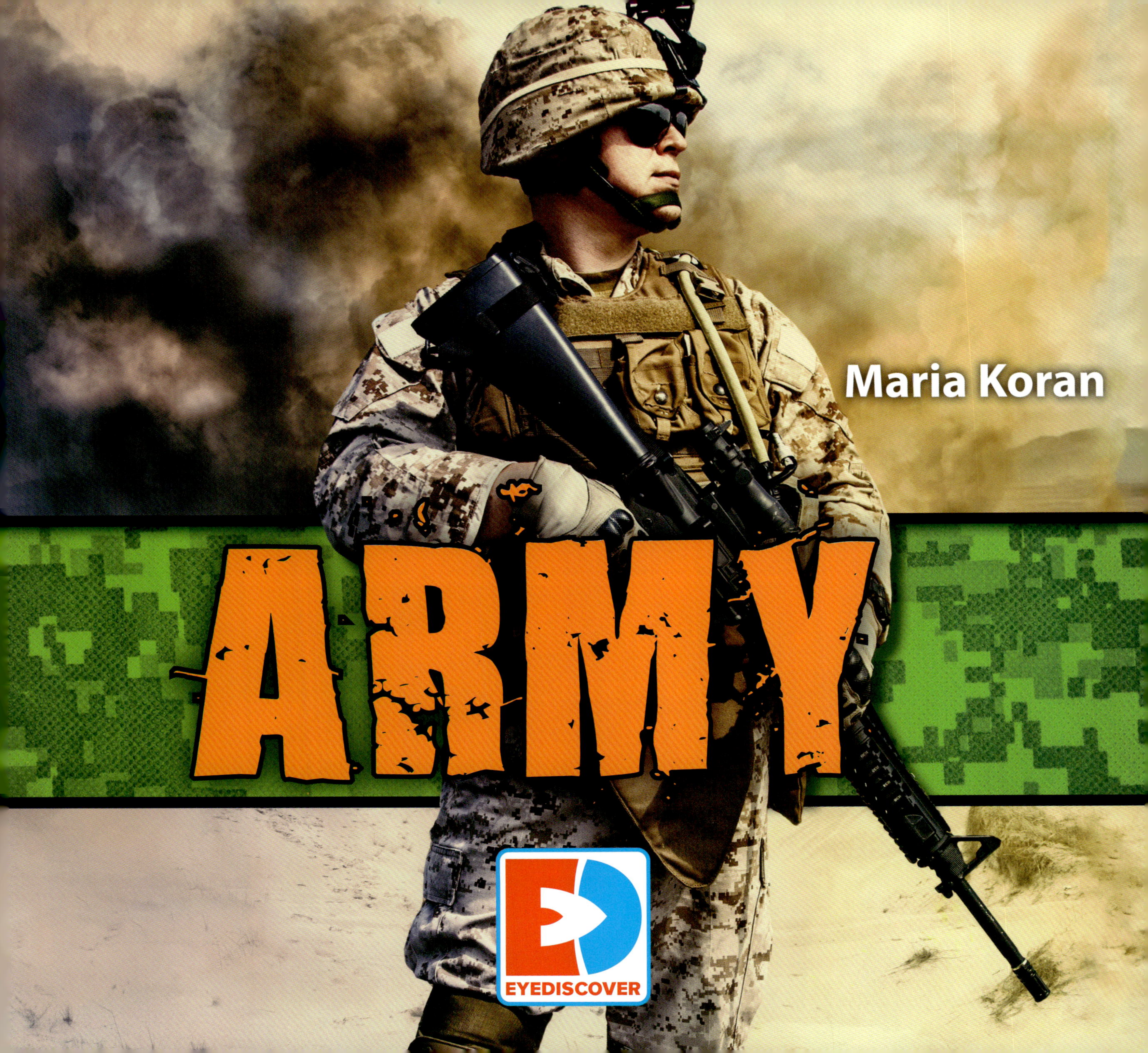
Maria Koran
ARMY
EYEDISCOVER

Go to **www.eyediscover.com** and enter this book's unique code.

BOOK CODE

AVS95472

EYEDISCOVER brings you optic readalongs that support active learning.

Published by AV² by Weigl
350 5th Avenue, 59th Floor New York, NY 10118
Website: www.eyediscover.com

Library of Congress Cataloging-in-Publication Data available on request

ISBN 978-1-7911-0768-0 (hardcover)

Printed in Guangzhou, China
1 2 3 4 5 6 7 8 9 0 23 22 21 20 19

072019
121818

Project Coordinator: John Willis
Designer: Mandy Christiansen and Sushant Deshpande

Weigl acknowledges Getty Images and iStock as the primary image suppliers for this title.

EYEDISCOVER provides enriched content, optimized for tablet use, that supplements and complements this book. EYEDISCOVER books strive to create inspired learning and engage young minds in a total learning experience.

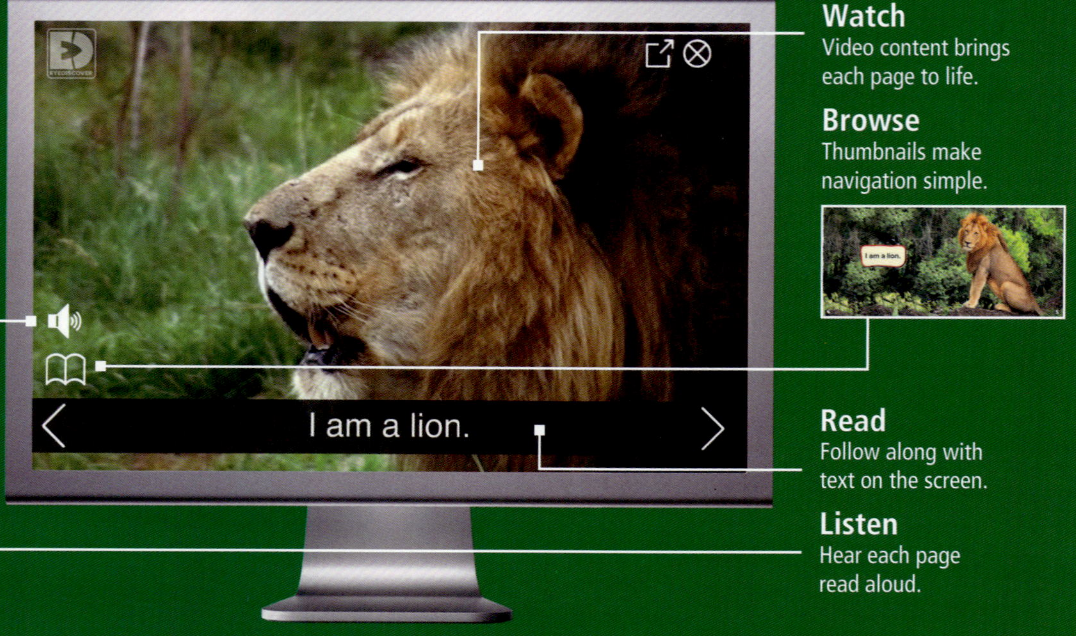

Watch
Video content brings each page to life.

Browse
Thumbnails make navigation simple.

Read
Follow along with text on the screen.

Listen
Hear each page read aloud.

Your EYEDISCOVER Optic Readalongs come alive with...

Audio
Listen to the entire book read aloud.

Video
High resolution videos turn each spread into an optic readalong.

OPTIMIZED FOR

- ✓ TABLETS
- ✓ WHITEBOARDS
- ✓ COMPUTERS
- ✓ AND MUCH MORE!

ARMY

In this book, you will learn about

- what it is
- what it does
- what tools it has

and much more!

An army is a group of soldiers. Its job is to keep a country safe.

The U.S. Army is more than 240 years old. It is older than the country it serves.

Today, the U.S. Army has about 1.3 million active duty members.

Training is important for soldiers. U.S. soldiers learn to shoot, move, and work as a team.

U.S. ARMY

Soldiers wear uniforms. Some uniforms help make a person harder to see.

The U.S. Army uses tanks. Their armor helps soldiers stay safe.

The U.S. Army has many helicopters. Some are used to help soldiers on the ground.

Other army helicopters are used to carry tools from one place to another.

FSC

Armies defend their country in many ways. The U.S. Army helps people after natural disasters.

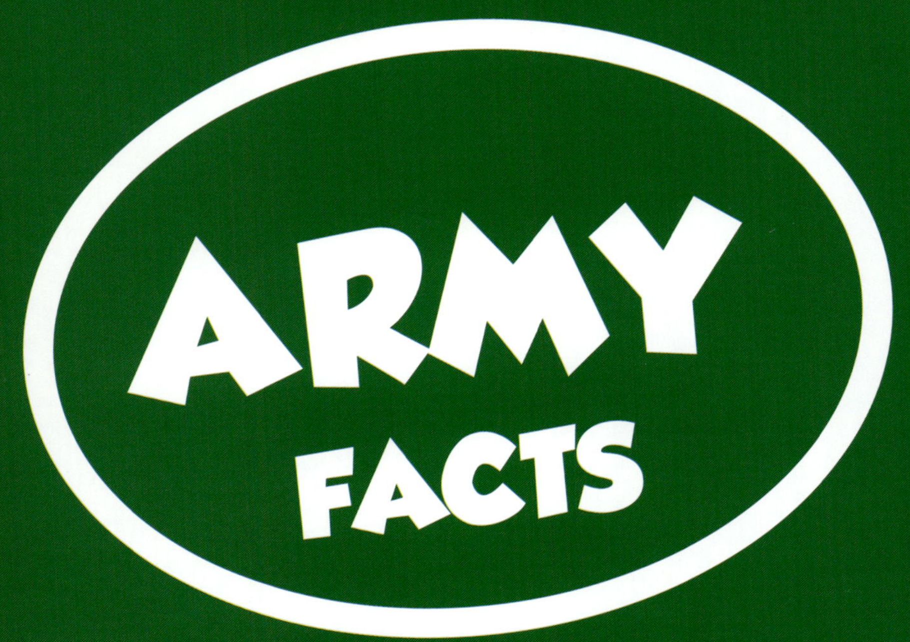

JUNE 14TH, 1775

is the official
birthday
of the U.S. Army.

The army is the
second
largest
employer in the
United States.

2 1 3

The U.S. Army uses **1 billion** gallons of **fuel** each year. (3.8 billion liters)

The **U.S. Army** owns more than **15 million** acres of land. (6 million hectares)

16 U.S. presidents have served in the army.

Military spending in the United States is more than **$600 billion** each year.

KEY WORDS

Research has shown that as much as 65 percent of all written material published in English is made up of 300 words. These 300 words cannot be taught using pictures or learned by sounding them out. They must be recognized by sight. This book contains 43 common sight words to help young readers improve their reading fluency and comprehension. This book also teaches young readers several important content words, such as proper nouns. These words are paired with pictures to aid in learning and improve understanding.

Page	Sight Words First Appearance
5	a, an, country, group, is, its, keep, of, to
6	it, more, old, than, the, years
9	about, has
10	and, as, for, important, learn, move, work
13	help, make, see, some
14	their, uses
17	are, many, on
18	another, carry, from, one, other, place
21	after, in, people, ways

Page	Content Words First Appearance
5	army, soldiers
6	U.S. Army
9	members
10	team, training
13	uniforms
14	armor, tanks
17	ground, helicopters
18	tools
21	natural disasters

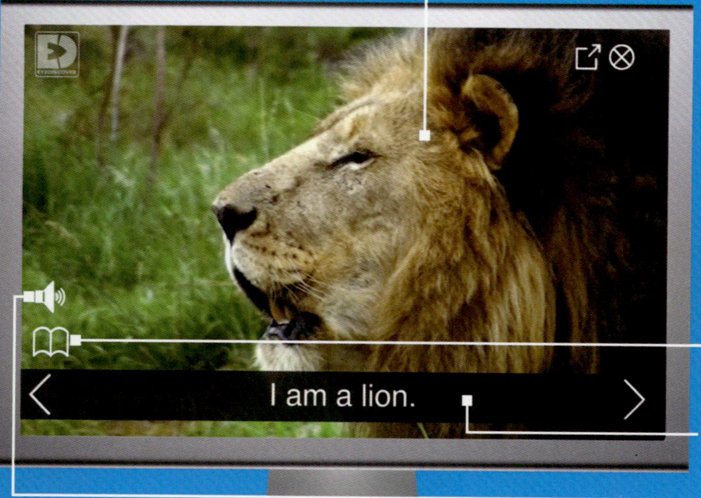

Watch
Video content brings each page to life.

Browse
Thumbnails make navigation simple.

Read
Follow along with text on the screen.

Listen
Hear each page read aloud.

Go to www.eyediscover.com and enter this book's unique code.

BOOK CODE

AVS95472